Fantasy Chronicles

Giants, Trolls, and Ogres

Shannon Knudsen

Lerner Publications Company · Minneapolis

Lerner Publications Company
A division of Lerner Publishing Group, Inc.
241 First Avenue North
Minneapolis, MN 55401 U.S.A.

Website address: www.lernerbooks.com

Library of Congress Cataloging-in-Publication Data

Knudsen, Shannon, 1971–
　　Giants, trolls, and ogres / by Shannon Knudsen.
　　　　p.　cm. — (Fantasy chronicles)
　　Includes bibliographical references and index.
　　ISBN 978-0-8225-9985-2 (lib. bdg. : alk. paper)
　　1. Giants—Juvenile literature. 2. Ghouls and ogres—Juvenile literature. 3. Trolls—Juvenile
literature.　I. Title.
　　GR560.K68 2010
　　398'.45—dc22   2009005212

Manufactured in the United States of America
1 2 3 4 5 6 – BP – 15 14 13 12 11 10

TABLE OF CONTENTS

❖ CHAPTER 1 ❖

Very Big and Very Scary 4

❖ CHAPTER 2 ❖

Giants of Europe 12

❖ CHAPTER 3 ❖

Around the Giant World 24

❖ CHAPTER 4 ❖

Giants among Us 36

Selected Bibliography 44
Further Reading and Websites 44
Movies 46
Index 47

VERY BIG AND VERY SCARY

Something is after you. Judging from the sound of its footsteps, it's something awfully large.

Branches slash your face as you rush through the woods. If you can just make it back to the cave where you and your friends are camping, maybe you can hide there. The ground starts to shake. The thing must be right behind you.

You glance over your shoulder to get a look at it. Mistake. You're not looking at the creature's head, as you expected. You're looking at its knees. Your eyes move up, up, up. You see an enormous clenched fist hurtling toward you. Fortunately for you, it blocks out the sunlight. So you can't see the pointy fangs of the ogre that's about to eat you.

People have always been fascinated by giants, ogres, and other huge beings. Giants are part of practically every human culture, from Ireland's powerful Finn McCool to China's hungry Begdu San. We tell stories about them, make movies about them, and even name our sports teams after them (just ask any New York Giants fan). It's no wonder that we think so highly of these high-reaching creatures. Giants look a lot like us, but their vast size makes them much more powerful than we are. That's probably why they're so scary—and so exciting.

So what makes a giant a giant? The answer is pretty simple. But there's a lot more to giants than you may have realized.

A giant happens upon a house in the wooded hills of Sweden.

Which Is Which?

Giants are humanoids—their shape is similar to a human being's. They're also big and strong. Really, really big and strong. There's no exact rule about how big and strong a humanoid has to be before it's a giant. Chances are, if it's big enough to make you look way up, you've entered giant territory.

Giants can be foul, nasty, and even violent. Remember the fairy tale "Jack and the Beanstalk"? That fellow who hollers "Fee, fi, fo, fum!" and tries to

Jack of "Jack and the Beanstalk" peers at the sleeping giant.

VERY BIG AND VERY SCARY

turn Jack into his supper is a perfect example. Some giants are much kinder, though. The character of Hagrid in J. K. Rowling's Harry Potter books is a half giant. He protects Harry and offers him information and advice. And how about the Jolly Green Giant? Nobody would buy groceries from a terrifying monster. But the Jolly Green Giant has been chuckling and selling vegetables for more than eighty years.

Giants come in many types. There are male giants and female giants, who are sometimes called giantesses. A giant could be a frost giant, a fire giant, a stone giant, a hill giant, or just a plain old giant. It depends on where it lives and what its body is made of.

The Jolly Green Giant *(left)* is a recognizable symbol in the American frozen foods section.

ARE GIANTS REAL?

For centuries the discovery of large animal fossils made people think that giants might be real. A mammoth's leg bone could be mistaken for the leg bone of a huge person, for example. But scientists have learned to analyze the shape of fossils they find. They are confident the fossils were once part of ancient animals, not giant humanoids.

Still, there are real-life cases of people growing to very large sizes. A medical condition called gigantism is usually the reason. Gigantism causes many health problems. In fact, people who have it usually don't live very long lives. According to the *Guinness World Records*, the tallest human being ever was Robert Pershing Wadlow (right). Doctors measured him in 1940, shortly before he died from an infection. They discovered he was 8 feet 11 inches (2.7 meters) tall. Wadlow was only twenty-two years old—and he was still growing.

Then there are ogres. They're giants with a particular fondness for eating people. Ogres are usually very hairy, smelly, and stupid.

An ogre gobbles up badly behaved children in this illustration from the 1500s by German artist Hans Weidlitz.

This Scandinavian troll puppet has the big nose that's typical of trolls. Trolls are frequently depicted in Scandinavian art and folktales.

A troll is a giant who lives underground. Trolls may or may not eat people. But they're almost always evil. Trolls appear most often in stories from the Scandinavian countries of northern Europe. They tend to have huge noses and small brains. (A troll can also be a tiny, woods-dwelling creature. But this book is about the big, creepy ones.)

Regardless of what you call them, these enormous humanoids have captured the imaginations of people for thousands of years. Let's get to know some giants from around the world to find out why.

CHAPTER 2

GIANTS OF EUROPE

Some of the oldest giant stories we know come
from the ancient Greeks. Greek mythology tells of
several groups of giants. One was the Titans. They
fought a war against the gods and goddesses of

Mount Olympus. The Titans were enormous and incredibly strong. But the Olympians proved to be more clever and more powerful, and they defeated the Titans. Zeus, the ruler of the gods, decided to punish the Titans. He imprisoned most of them in Tartarus. It was a deep, dark pit at the bottom of the underworld, the home of the dead.

One Titan, Atlas, had been a leader in the war. So Zeus wanted to give him a harder punishment. He forced Atlas to hold up the sky above the earth. This terrible burden would have lasted forever. But Atlas became a mountain range when he saw the head of the monster Medusa. Her gaze turned all living things to stone, including Atlas.

Another Titan, Prometheus, suffered more than Atlas. Prometheus didn't fight against the Olympians. In fact, he helped them defeat the other Titans. But later, he angered Zeus by stealing fire from Mount Olympus and giving it to humans. Zeus punished him by chaining him to a rock. Every day, a vulture flew down and snacked on the Titan's liver. Since the Titans were immortal, Prometheus couldn't die. He could only suffer. Every night, his liver grew back. And the vulture returned the next day for a fresh bite.

In this illustration from the 1800s, the Titan Prometheus suffers his punishment from Zeus.

The cyclopses were another group of Greek giants. They were far uglier and nastier than the Titans. A cyclops had one large eye in the middle of its forehead. And it had remarkable brute strength. Cyclopses liked to eat people. That made them ogres as well as giants.

The most famous cyclops story appears in *The Odyssey*. This epic tale was written by the Greek poet Homer some time between 750 and 650 B.C. The hero Odysseus is returning home from the Trojan War (ca. 1200s or 1100s B.C.) with his men. Their ship lands on the Island of the Cyclopes. As the men explore a cave, its owner returns. He is the mighty cyclops Polyphemus, and he blocks the entrance of the cave with a stone. Then he promptly eats two of the men, lifting them up and smashing them against the ground to kill them.

The next day, Polyphemus eats two more men. Then he takes his sheep out to graze. The cave is still blocked with the stone. It's much too heavy for the men to move. But Odysseus makes a plan. Polyphemus returns with the sheep and has another human supper. Then Odysseus gives him strong wine. Soon the cyclops is drunk and sleepy. The men sharpen his club into a point and jab it into his eye. Polyphemus is enraged. But since he cannot see, the men manage to dodge his blows.

When morning comes, Polyphemus must let his sheep out to graze again. He carefully feels each one. He is afraid his prisoners might ride out of the cave on top of the sheep. Imagine his shock when he discovers that the men have escaped anyway! The clever Odysseus and his men tied themselves *underneath* the sheep. Polyphemus couldn't feel them.

The blinded cyclops
Polyphemus tries to find
Odysseus and his men.

Tall Tales from Scandinavia

The mythology of Scandinavia is often called Norse mythology. And it gives giants a starring role. According to Norse mythology, at the beginning of creation, the world was frozen. Beams of fire from the far south started to melt the frost. A vast giant called Ymir was created by the melting water. Next, a huge cow was formed. Ymir drank the cow's milk. Other giants emerged from his body. They became the frost giants.

That was just the start. The cow licked the ice for nourishment and uncovered a man called Buri. He became the first god. Buri eventually had three grandsons named Odin, Ve, and Vili. These three brothers became alarmed at the growing number of giants. They decided to kill Ymir.

German artist Emil Doepler created this illustration of the Scandinavian giant Ymir.

So much blood flowed from Ymir's corpse that all the giants except two were drowned. Odin and his brothers then used Ymir's body to create Earth. His blood made up the oceans. His teeth and bones became rocks. His hair became trees, and his brains became clouds. His skull became the sky. Finally, the brothers made Ymir's eyebrows into the place where humans would live. It was called Midgard.

The two remaining giants had many children. This new race of giants made plenty of trouble for the gods. But sometimes gods and giants married and had families. And one giant, Loki, became a god himself. Loki could change his shape into any living thing. He soon had a reputation for telling lies and tricking other gods. Sometimes he helped them, but just as often, he caused trouble. He even caused the death of Balder, the god of light.

Loki was smart, but most Scandinavian giants weren't. In

In one tale, Loki is captured and chained under a dripping venemous snake. Loki's violent thrashing shook the earth, giving rise to earthquakes.

many cases, their victims could use their wits to save themselves, just as Odysseus did. The Norwegian fairy tale "The Three Billy Goats Gruff" gives an example. This popular story was first written down in 1845. But it had been passed on by storytellers for generations before that.

Three goats, all named Gruff, must cross a bridge to reach the grass on the other side. But the bridge is guarded by a terrible troll. It devours anyone who comes along. The youngest goat goes

first. When he meets the troll, he explains that his brothers are on the way. They're much bigger than he is, he says. So the troll should wait and eat them. That sounds reasonable to the troll. He lets the youngest Gruff go. Next comes the middle goat. He uses the same argument. His bigger brother will be along soon. The troll will get a much better meal if he eats the largest goat. Once again, the troll agrees to wait.

Along comes the biggest of the billy goats Gruff. He promptly butts the troll with his huge horns. The troll sails over the side of the bridge and is never seen again. The clever billy goats can cross the bridge whenever they like.

English and French Giants

Giants make an early appearance in English lore too. The legendary King Arthur was said to be a giant slayer, for example. Scholars who study the past think that Arthur was a real person. But many stories that are told about him aren't true. The tale of the giant Retho is one of these.

Retho had defeated many kings in combat. The kings had all worn beards, and Retho had found a strange use for them. He had a cloak made entirely out of the kings' beards. Arthur had a beard too. So Retho sent him a message instructing him to rip it off and send it along. It would be added to the cloak. And since Arthur was such a great king, Retho added, he would make sure to put his beard at the top of the cloak, above the others.

King Arthur fights the giant Retho. Arthur emerges victorious against his oversized opponent.

Arthur was not impressed. He challenged Retho to a duel. The giant proved to be the strongest opponent he had ever faced. But Arthur won. He took both the hairy cloak and Retho's own beard as trophies.

Not all Europe's giants were as creepy as Retho. Some very funny giants appeared in the work of a French writer, François Rabelais. Beginning in the 1530s, he wrote several books about two huge humanoids, Gargantua and his son, Pantagruel. The adventures of this pair are often silly. That's because their main goals in life are to have fun and tell naughty jokes. For example, one of their quests is to figure out what material makes the best toilet paper! Rabelais also used his giants to poke fun at religion and government. That made some people quite angry with him. But many more loved his sense of humor.

Causeway Builder

One of the greatest heroes of Irish folklore is a giant warrior known as Finn McCool. His skill as a warrior was unmatched. But his incredible size and strength couldn't be beaten either. Finn is said to have created several geographical features in and around Ireland. One of them is the Giant's Causeway. This raised road lies on the coast of Northern Ireland. The Giant's Causeway is made up of forty thousand columns of a rock called basalt *(below)*. Scientists believe that the columns were formed by the eruption of an ancient volcano. But Irish storytellers say that Finn built the causeway as a series of stepping-stones across the sea to Scotland!

Giants played an appropriately big part in a book called *Gulliver's Travels*. It was written in 1726 by Jonathan Swift, who was born in Ireland. His novel tells the story of Lemuel Gulliver, a regular person who travels to several unusual worlds. One of them is Brobdingnag, the home of giants who are 900 feet (274 m) tall. Everything in Brobdingnag is enormous. The only

Gulliver plays the part of the giant when he visits the land of the tiny Lilliputians. In the mid-1900s, Italian comic-book artist Nadir Quinto illustrated this scene from *Gulliver's Travels*.

exception is Gulliver, who ends up in the service of the nation's queen. She has a tiny house built for him and takes him wherever she goes. So how does Gulliver make it back home? His house is captured by a giant eagle. It carries him to the ocean and drops him. Human sailors find him and bring him home.

Gulliver's Travels became extremely popular. It remains one of the most famous books written in the English language. In fact, it has even given us new words. The word *Brobdingnagian* can be used to describe anything that's incredibly large.

CHAPTER 3

AROUND THE GIANT WORLD

As in Europe, people from around the world have their fair share of giant tales. One of the most famous North American giants is surely the American lumberjack Paul Bunyan. Tall tales about Paul became well known during the early 1900s. But loggers had been telling them over campfires long before that. Paul was so big that he used a fully grown pine tree to comb his beard. His big blue ox, Babe, needed a watering hole. So Paul dug Lake Michigan. Forest fires were no trouble for Paul, either. He just stamped them out with his boots.

The mythical Paul Bunyan carries a log through the forests of North America.

Paul Bunyan is one of the few friendly and helpful giants in North American lore. Native American peoples throughout Canada and the northern United States have told stories for centuries about an ogre called the Windigo. This monster has claws that are more than a foot (0.3 m) long and rows of pointy, jagged teeth. His eyes are yellow, and they bulge out of his head like a fish's eyes. Each of his feet is more than

3 feet (0.9 m) long. The feet end in a single toe, with a toenail as sharp as a knife.

As if all that weren't scary enough, the Windigo has a terrible goal in life. He loves to eat people. His appetite for flesh is so great that he has no lips. Why? Because he's chewed them off! He'll settle for mushrooms and moss if he can't find a tasty human to snack on. But then he'll be hungrier than ever.

The best defense against a Windigo is to watch out for whirlwinds (small windstorms) and

The Windigo of Native American folklore travels as fast as a windstorm and feeds on human flesh.

tornadoes. His approach is so fast and violent that he creates storms as he approaches. The one and only way to kill a Windigo is to burn him to death. A Windigo's heart is made of ice. So fire will melt it and destroy the beast for good.

An Inuit woman carries her baby on her back. Inuit folklore tells of a terrifying ogre who tricked mothers into letting her take care of their babies. Then, look out!

The chilly lands of the northern regions of North America have given rise to other terrifying giants and ogres. The Inuit of the eastern Hudson Bay area of Canada gave a warning to the mothers of newborn babies. Be careful if a stranger offers to babysit, they cautioned. The stranger might be Tammatuyuq. This tricky female ogre appears in traditional stories. Her way of finding food was simple. She would help tired new mothers take care of their infants. Once a mother started to trust her, Tammatuyuq waited until the mom became distracted. Then she stole the baby. Back in her lair, she pierced the child's head with a needle and sucked out the blood.

The warmer regions of the American Southwest have giants too. A remarkable giant of this area's Native American legends is

Yeitso. The Hopi and Navajo peoples describe him as being especially terrifying because he is covered with scales. He hunted people for food. And he caught plenty of them. Two young heroes, twins named Nayenygami and Tobadzistsini, decided they had to destroy Yeitso. They traveled through the sky and asked the sun god to help them. He gave them powerful arrows made of rainbows, sunbeams, and lightning. The twins used these weapons to kill Yeitso. They saved their people from his terrible appetite.

This volcanic outcropping in New Mexico is called Cabezon, a Spanish word that means "Great Head." According to Native American legend, when Yeitso's head was chopped off, it fell here and turned to stone.

African Ogres

The Sotho people of southeastern Africa tell stories of Kholomodumo, an ancient ogre. Kholomodumo had been part of the world since the beginning of creation. His appetite was so huge that he ate every single human being except one. This clever woman managed to hide herself. While she was hiding, she gave birth to twin boys. When the boys matured, they decided to track down Kholomodumo and kill him. With their dog's help, they succeeded in their quest to defeat the ogre. Once the ogre died, all the people the monster had consumed came forth from its body. The world was safe and full of humans once again.

In western Africa, the Ashanti and Tschwi peoples describe a creepy kind of ogre. The male ogres are called Sasabonsam, while

These men are from the Sotho group in southeastern Africa. Much African folklore contains stories of giants and ogres.

the females are called Shamantin. Both are tall and thin. They have long legs and feet that point both forward and backward. Their skin is the color of blood. That's probably because their favorite food is human blood.

Sasabonsam and Shamantin have a clever way of capturing prey. They lurk in trees. From a high branch, they dangle their legs downward. Their bizarre feet rest on the ground. They look like tree roots. When a person passes beneath the tree, the ogre uses its feet to grab the poor traveler. How can you tell which trees may be hiding Sasabonsam and Shamantin? Study the ground near the roots. If it's red, stay away! That's where these terrifying ogres wipe off the leftover blood from their meal.

Asian Giants

A Chinese giant called Begdu San was far less dangerous than many. But he caused trouble without intending to. He began his life in northern Korea. His appetite was so enormous that he ate all the plants for as far as anyone could see. As a result, he grew so tall that his body blocked out the sunlight. His shadow left the land in darkness. The people forced Begdu San to go live in the mountains to the north. That worked well for a while. But soon he had eaten all the trees and drained the rivers of water. Off he went to eastern China. There he began to drink the ocean. But the salty water made him sick. As Begdu San's huge body crashed to the ground, it formed a mountain range.

The Southeast Asian country of Indonesia has its own peaceful giant. This giant turned out to be much more helpful than Begdu San. Wikramadatta ruled as king of all the giants on the island of Java. He was known for his wisdom. One day he observed that the humans of Java had become very violent. He demanded that the human king, Jamajaya, send him a gift of all the weapons on the island.

It's probably pretty difficult to say no when the king of the giants asks you for a present! King Jamajaya agreed and gathered all the arms on Java. He sent them to Wikramadatta, who kept them away from the people. From that time on, peace reigned throughout the land.

The Chukchee people live in the freezing cold land of Siberia. It is in the northern part of the nation of Russia. The Chukchee live by hunting and herding reindeer. They're often on the move. Maybe

The Chukchee people of Siberia depend on reindeer for food, clothing, and shelter. One of their legends tells of an ogre who stalks hunters.

that's why one of their scariest ogres is a hunter of travelers. This ogre's snout makes noises that sound like music. It can also wail like a person in distress to attract the attention of wanderers. Of course, anyone who falls for the ogre's lures will become its next meal.

Another enemy of the Chukchee is the gigantic Re'kkeñ. This type of troll eats nothing but people. It has the body of a bear and terrible fangs. Worse still, Re'kkeñ are quite intelligent. They can use canoes and set traps made of nets. They live in underground homes, venturing out to find prey. At night their fires burn a bloodred color.

The land inside the borders of Syria, Turkey, and Iraq was once the home of the Hurrian people, as well as many others. The Hurrians lived in this region, then called Mesopotamia, from about 2500 to 1600 B.C. Their mythology included the story of the stone giant Ullikummi. Made of green quartz, Ullikummi couldn't see or hear. It was neither female nor male. Yet it grew and grew and grew. At last, its body forced the earth downward into the oceans. It pushed the sky upward toward outer space too. The entire world might have been destroyed by Ullikummi. But the god Ea cut off its feet. Ullikummi crashed into the ocean. The waters covered its body forever.

Australia and the South Pacific

The native peoples of Australia have a legend that begins with a man named Djarapa. Long ago, he carved a tree into a Wulgaru, a wooden giant. He took great care with his work. Djarapa made joints that could move, and he made teeth from pieces of flint. He gave the Wulgaru pebbles for eyes and hair from his own wife's head. Finally, it was almost finished. Djarapa chanted all the spells he could think of to bring the giant to life. But nothing worked.

The frustrated man gave the Wulgaru a hard kick and stomped off. Moments later, he heard loud noises that seemed to match his footsteps. He looked back. Sure enough, it was his Wulgaru! But the pebble eyes looked very angry. Djarapa ran as fast as he could. The Wulgaru kept up with him. Djarapa turned at a bend in the path and hid behind a large tree. The Wulgaru stayed on the path. It walked straight into the river, and emerged on the other side!

Djarapa hurried to his village and warned his people about the Wulgaru. But the giant proved to be indestructible. According to legend, at night he still comes to eat those who break the law. But those who have done nothing wrong are safe.

Fiji is a nation of islands that lies east of Australia in the South Pacific Ocean. It has a rich tradition of storytelling. Flaming Teeth was a legendary ogre of the island of Rotuma. The ogre was named for a special weapon he had. His teeth were spikes of fire almost as big as mountains. When he opened his mouth, flames came out. And he could burn his victims to death as he ate them!

No one could hide for long from this powerful hunter. After many people had died, two men decided they had to stop the ogre. So they set a trap. Inside a house, they placed a huge rock in the rafters, the beams that hold up the roof. Then they tricked

Flaming Teeth into running into the house. The men pushed the rock onto his head, crushing him. Before his mouth grew cold, the people brought torches and lit them from the remaining flames. And that's how the ancient Fijians came to have fire.

REMOVABLE GIANT PARTS

Another Fijian giant is Tui Delai Gau. He lives on Gau Island. His magical powers and size make him a particularly unusual giant. When he wants to fish for food, he doesn't need to go to the shore himself. He just sends his hands there to do the work without the rest of his body. (The hands can walk along on their fingers.) If Tui Delai Gau can't see quite as far as he needs to, he can solve that problem easily too. He simply removes his head and holds it high, turning it in whatever direction he wants to look. Fortunately for the people of Gau Island, this gifted giant likes human beings. He taught the island's early inhabitants how to use a spade to dig up the ground to plant seeds. He also taught them how to cook.

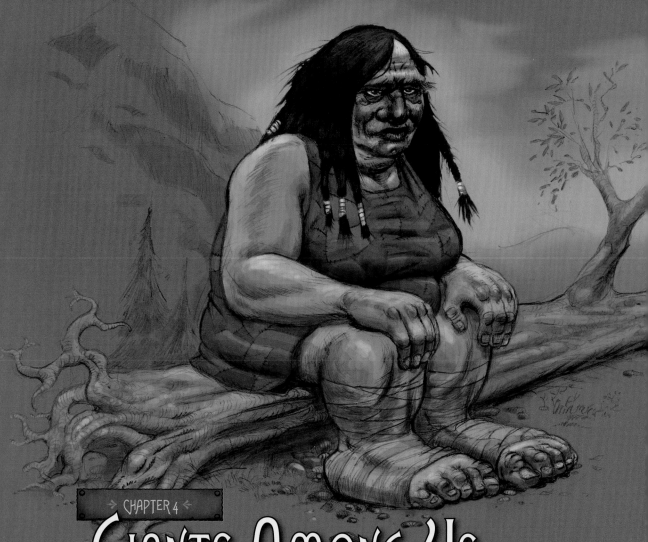

CHAPTER 4

GIANTS AMONG US

Myths and other old stories are interesting enough. But giants aren't only a thing of the past. Modern readers and audiences can't get enough of them. Many modern writers have explored the idea that being gigantic doesn't have to mean being scary or mean.

There are no giants of the usual kind in Roald Dahl's 1967 book *James and the Giant Peach*. But there are plenty of giant creatures. A bag of magic crystals causes a ladybug, an earthworm, a centipede, and several other animals to grow to enormous size. A peach grows along with them, and they make their home inside the peach's pit. A normal-sized boy, James, joins them. The appearance of his enormous companions terrifies James at first. But they turn out to be friendly and intelligent. This popular children's book was made into a movie in 1996.

Roald Dahl wrote another story about giants, The *BFG*. It was published in 1982. Most of this book's giants are like the ones of myth and legend. They're ugly, mean, and hungry. And their favorite food is people, especially kids. They have names like the Fleshlumpeater and the Bloodbottler. But one giant is different. He's the BFG, which stands for "Big Friendly Giant." He helps people by sending them good dreams and destroying bad ones.

Giants are both nasty and nice in *The Giants and the Joneses* by Julia Donaldson. This 2005 book reverses the plot of "Jack and the Beanstalk." A young giant girl named Jumbeelia climbs down to the earth to look for human beings. She brings back the three Jones children and keeps them as pets. Jumbeelia is fairly kind to her "iggly plops." (That's what giants call humans in the book.) But Jumbeelia's brother becomes jealous. When he gets his hands on the Joneses, things turn dangerous. The Jones siblings must figure out how to escape and return to safety before their luck runs out.

Trolls have their place in modern stories too. Alan Snow's 2006 book *Here Be Monsters!* features boxtrolls. These tall, sharp-toothed giants are unusually shy. So they lurk inside cardboard boxes. They love anything with mechanical or moving parts. And they love to steal.

What would you do if a troll showed up on your doorstep, looking for a place to stay? That's the problem Samuel Blink has to solve in *Samuel Blink and the Runaway Troll*. This 2008 book by Matt Haig tells the story of Troll-Son. He runs away from his home in the forest and tries to bunk with Samuel. Troll-Son is a one-eyed troll, and he's especially smelly. But he'll be in for an unspeakable punishment if Samuel sends him back to the forest.

How about ogres? The most famous modern ogre is surely Shrek, a huge, green fellow with a potbelly. Shrek has bad

manners and a bad temper to match. He grumbles a lot and likes to burp and fart. But

Mike Myers plays the voice of Shrek *(above)* **on the silver screen.**

where his friends and his beloved Fiona are concerned, Shrek is a big softy. (He doesn't eat people, either, unlike the ogres of myths and folktales.)

As the star of a popular animated movie series, Shrek has millions of fans. Most of them don't know that he started out as a book character, not a movie monster. William Steig wrote and illustrated the picture book *Shrek!* (1990). The way he tells it, Shrek was uglier than both his mom and his dad put together. And he was so nasty that any snake that bit him died instantly.

Huge Heroes

Shrek isn't the only big green guy to make a strong impression in our culture. The Hulk has been popular for close to half a century. He began as a comic-book character created by Stan Lee and Jack Kirby in the early 1960s. Hulk comics have been published ever since.

The Hulk is the second identity of Bruce Banner. He's a scientist whose body was damaged by radiation from a bomb he was testing. When he becomes stressed or angry, he transforms into a huge, green giant. As the Hulk, Bruce has superhuman strength and can leap hundreds of miles at a time. (Once he almost leaped from the ground into orbit around Earth!) Because he often does physical damage and is overcome by rage, the Hulk is constantly misunderstood. The character of the Hulk is so well liked by fans that he has starred in several movies and TV series, as well as video games.

One of the Hulk's rivals in comic books is another giant superhero. The Thing made

The Incredible Hulk made his debut to comic-book audiences in 1962. He's still going strong in comic books and on the big screen.

his start in 1961 in the comic *The Fantastic Four.* It was another creation of Stan Lee and Jack Kirby. In this comic, Ben Grimm is the pilot of an experimental rocket. It has a crew of four, including Ben. When a cosmic ray storm exposes them to radiation, all four crew members get special powers. Ben becomes enormous. He grows an orange skin with rocky plates, and he takes on the name the Thing. The Thing joins his friends in fighting for the forces of good.

The Hulk and the Thing have appeared together many times in issues of *The Fantastic Four, The Incredible Hulk*, and other comics. Both the Thing and the Hulk have good intentions. Since the Hulk often grows large, he ends up competing with the Thing. Their huge size makes them a good match, but the Hulk tends to get the upper hand.

GIANT COMIC-BOOK VILLAINS

Some comic-book giants are villains. Consider Giganta, who can change her size from normal to several hundred feet tall whenever she likes. She's been an enemy of Wonder Woman for several decades of comic-book and TV history. Then there's Juggernaut, a bad guy from the *X-Men* series. His superhuman strength can knock over skyscrapers and even cause trouble for the Hulk.

A heroic giant makes a huge difference in *The Princess Bride.* William Goldman wrote this book in 1973. In 1987 it was

Fezzik, played by André the Giant, dwarfs Princess Buttercup (Robin Wright) in the 1987 film *The Princess Bride.*

made into a movie, which remains popular. People love the story partly for the character of the giant Fezzik, played in the movie by André the Giant. Fezzik is big enough and strong enough to kidnap Princess Buttercup. A mysterious man in black chases after them. Fezzik has a chance to kill the man by hiding behind a rock and ambushing him. But Fezzik doesn't like hurting people. So he just tosses a rock to warn the man in black and shows himself.

Later, Fezzik changes sides. He joins forces with the man in black to rescue Buttercup from the evil Prince Humperdinck. Fezzik scares away the dozens of soldiers guarding the castle. This gentle giant even brings horses just in time to make the perfect escape.

Gaming with Giants

Video games have become a wonderful way for people to express their fascination with huge monsters. In the *EverQuest* series, players can create characters that are either trolls or ogres. Various kinds of giants challenge players as enemies too. *Final Fantasy XI* includes the Australian giant Wulgaru and the Hurrian giant Ullikummi as enemies. And of course, there are video game versions of many of the stories and characters you've read about in this book, including the Hulk.

Perhaps the most original use of giants in a video game is in the 2005 stunner *Shadow of the Colossus*. A colossus is something that is almost unimaginably large. That's certainly true of the enemies in *Shadow of the Colossus*. These sixteen giants are huge. The player must climb and explore each giant to find its weaknesses. Then the player must kill it, while avoiding the giant's attacks.

Whether you experience giants through books, movies, games, or all three, chances are you won't forget these remarkable humanoids. Without giants, our culture and our imaginations would start to feel pretty small indeed. Lucky for us, the big fellows and gals of the fantasy world are much too enormous to ever disappear.

Selected Bibliography

Davidson, Hilda Ellis, and Anna Chaudhri, eds. *Supernatural Enemies.*
Durham, NC: Carolina Academic Press, 2001.

Gilmore, David D. *Monsters: Evil Beings, Mythical Beasts, and
All Manner of Imaginary Terrors.* Philadelphia: University of
Pennsylvania Press, 2003.

Rose, Carol. *Giants, Monsters, and Dragons.* New York: W. W. Norton
& Co., 2001.

Rose, H. J. *A Handbook of Greek Mythology.* New York: Dutton & Co.,
1959.

Stephens, Walter. *Giants in Those Days.* Lincoln: University of
Nebraska Press, 1989.

Further Reading and Websites

Books

Berk, Ari. *The Secret History of Giants.* Somerville, MA: Candlewick
Press, 2008.
This book describes giants throughout history, including the Titans
and the biblical giant Goliath. What do giants carry in their huge
sacks? What kinds of jobs do they do? The answers are all here. A
map also points out locations where giants live.

Jolley, Dan. *Odysseus: Escaping Poseidon's Curse.* Minneapolis:
Graphic Universe, 2007.
The Graphic Myths and Legends series offers retellings of stories from

cultures around the world in a comic-book format. This book describes how the Greek hero Odysseus tried to lead his men home after the Trojan War. It includes their encounter with the cyclops Polyphemus as well as many other adventures. Additional material includes a glossary, map, index, and an explanation of how the book was created.

Limke, Jeff. *Thor and Loki: In the Land of Giants*. Minneapolis: Graphic Universe, 2007.
Another title in the Graphic Myths and Legends series, this book takes on a Norse myth in which Thor and Loki have a disagreement. Will strength always beat a quick wit, or are brains enough to defeat brawn? To solve their argument, the god of thunder and the trickster journey to the land of giants, where they find more than they expected.

Websites

Guinness World Records
http://www.guinnessworldrecords.com
This site is the online version of the best-selling book series in the world. Here viewers can keep up with the latest data on the world's tallest people and much more.

Here Be Monsters!
http://www.here-be-monsters.com
Author and artist Alan Snow re-created the world of his book *Here Be Monsters!* on this site. Viewers can download wallpaper, posters, and a blueprint for creating a model of the theater featured in the story.

SurLaLune Fairy Tales: The Annotated Three Billy Goats Gruff
   http://www.surlalunefairytales.com/billygoats/index.html
   This site retells tales such as "The Three Billy Goats Gruff." But the
   most unusual part of this site is the annotations. These brief additions
   explain unusual words or offer facts to help readers understand
   different aspects of the story. Click on the small numbers that appear
   throughout the text to read the annotations.

Movies

The Incredible Hulk. DVD. Beverly Hills, CA: Marvel Studios, 2008.
   In this film, Bruce Banner tries desperately to control his
   transformations into the Hulk. But the U.S. military is determined
   to capture the Hulk, so Banner is constantly in danger. To make
   matters worse, one of his pursuers mutates into a terrifying monster,
   the Abomination.

The Princess Bride. DVD. Los Angeles: Twentieth Century Fox, 1987.
   Start with a girl named Buttercup and a boy named Westley. Add
   romance, sword fights, a kidnapping, and a giant named Fezzik who
   likes rhyming words. What do you get? Fans would say the result is
   one of the funniest action-adventure movies of all time.

Shrek. DVD. Universal City, CA: DreamWorks SKG, 2001.
   When Shrek's home is invaded by noisy fairy-tale creatures, Shrek
   sets out to solve the problem and finds himself on an accidental quest
   to save a princess. This animated movie launched a hugely popular
   film series and became the first to win a newly created Oscar
   category, Best Animated Feature.

Index

Arthur, King, 19
Ashanti, 30
Atlas, 13

Begdu San, 5, 31–32
Bunyan, Paul, 24–26

Chukchee, 32–33
cyclops, 14,

Dahl, Roald, 37–38
Djarpa, 33–34

Fantastic Four, The, 41
fossils, giant, 9,

Giant's Causeway, 21
Giganta, 41
gigantism, 9
Gulliver's Travels, 22–23

Incredible Hulk, 40

"Jack and the Beanstalk," 7–8
Jamajaya, King, 32
Jolly Green Giant, 8

Kholomodumo, 30

Loki, 17

McCool, Finn, 5, 21

Native Americans, 28–29
Norse mythology, 16–18

Odysseus, 14–15
ogre, 10

Polyphemus, 14–15
Princess Bride, The, 42
Prometheus, 13–14

Re'kkeñ, 33
Retho, 19

Shrek, 38–39
Sotho, 30

Tammatuyuq, 28
"Three Billy Goats Gruff, The," 18–19
Titan, 12–13
troll, 11, 19
Tschwi, 30

Ullikummi, 33

video games, 43

Wadlow, Robert Pershing, 9
Wikramadatta, 32
Windigo, 26–27
Wulgaru, 33–34

Yeitso, 29
Ymir, 16–17

About the Author

Shannon Knudsen has written thirty books for kids on subjects ranging from orangutans to the life of Thomas Edison. She lives in Tucson, Arizona, with a cat, a dog, and several kinds of cactuses.

Photo Acknowledgments

The images in this book are used with the permission of: Mary Evans Picture Library/Everett Collection, pp. 1, 10, 16, 17; © John Bauer/The Bridgeman Art Library/Getty Images, p. 6; Look and Learn/The Bridgeman Art Library, pp. 7, 20, 22; © Todd Strand/Independent Picture Service, p. 8; Everett Collection, p. 9; © Lee Snider/The Image Works, p. 11; © akg-images/The Image Works, p. 14; © Anatoly Sapronenkov/SuperStock, p. 15; © Digital Vision/Getty Images, p. 21; © Blue Lantern Studio/CORBIS, p. 26; © Svensson/Fortean/TopFoto/The Image Works, p. 27; © 2nd Alan King/Alamy, p. 28; © Tim Pleasant/Dreamstime.com, p. 29; © Westend61/SuperStock, p. 30; © Pat O'Hara/CORBIS, p. 32; © DreamWorks/courtesy Everett Collection, p. 39; © Universal/courtesy Everett Collection, p. 40; © 20th Century Fox Film Corp. All rights reserved/courtesy Everett Collection, p. 42. Illustrations © Bill Hauser/Independent Picture Service, pp. 4-5, 12-13, 18, 24-25, 36-37. All page backgrounds illustrated by © Bill Hauser/Independent Picture Service.

Front cover: Illustration by Devon Cady-Lee © 2009 Saul Zaentz Co. All rights reserved. ™ Saul Zaentz Co. under license to Turbine, Inc.